Kramer, Alan
How to make a chemical
volcano.

CUP

HOW TO MAKE
A CHEMICAL VOLCANO
AND
OTHER MYSTERIOUS
EXPERIMENTS

ALAN KRAMER

HOW TO MAKE A CHEMICAL VOLCANO
AND OTHER MYSTERIOUS EXPERIMENTS

FRANKLIN WATTS / 1989
NEW YORK / LONDON / TORONTO / SYDNEY

Illustrations by Paul Harvey / Diagrams by Kathie Kelleher

Library of Congress Cataloging-in-Publication Data

Kramer, Alan.
    How to make a chemical volcano and other mysterious experiments /
by Alan Kramer.
        p.   cm.
    Bibliography: p.
    Includes index.
    Summary: The thirteen-year-old author presents twenty-nine
experiments using household chemicals and materials that demonstrate
a physical or chemical principle while seeming like tricks.
    ISBN 0-531-15120-4.—ISBN 0-531-10771-X (lib. bdg.)
    1. Chemistry—Experiments—Juvenile literature. [1. Chemistry—
Experiments. 2. Experiments. 3. Children's writings.] I. Title.
QD38.K73 1989
542—dc20   89-8994 CIP AC

CONTENTS

HOW TO MAKE
A CHEMICAL VOLCANO
AND
OTHER MYSTERIOUS
EXPERIMENTS

IN MEMORY OF A
VERY SPECIAL MAN:
MY GRANDFATHER,
JOHN LEROY SIEGRIST

INTRODUCTION

Hello, I am a thirteen-year-old student named Alan Kramer. I like chemistry, and I know you must like it too, or else you wouldn't be reading this book.

Making things fizz and explode is lots of fun. But, that's not all there is to chemistry. It is important in our everyday lives. Without chemistry there would be no automobile tires, no paint, or even this paper and the ink on it.

Many chemistry books require the use of chemicals for their experiments. This can be very expensive. It can also be very difficult to find a store that sells chemicals. Only a few hobby shops sell chemicals and then the choice is very limited. One of the reasons it is difficult to find stores that sell chemicals is because of the dangerous properties in many of the chemicals.

For these reasons all of the experiments in this book, with the exception of one, can be done with things that can be found in your home. The only experiment that requires chemicals is "The Mysterious Changeable Weatherman," which uses cobalt chloride. Fortunately, this chemical can be found in a hobby shop. Another experiment, "The Mystical Mothball Tree," can be done with moth-flakes or with benzoic acid, which is another chemical usually available at a hobby shop that sells chemicals.

Let's get on with the instructions for using this book and instructions for gathering, storing, and using your supplies. All of these instructions are very important in order to perform the mysterious experiments safely.

This book can be more fun if you pretend you are a "Detective of Chemistry." I will be your faithful assistant and guide you in solving the mysteries of chemistry. Remember, chemistry is fun!

HOW TO USE THIS BOOK

In this book you will see some special symbols and words. Here is an example of some of the words and symbols:

CAUTION

This means that the chemical you are using is either poisonous, flammable, or may cause a stain. So *watch out*! Whenever the word CAUTION is used within an experiment, it means that you *must* have adult supervision.

CHEMICAL NAME
(example:
sodium chloride)

This is used to help you learn the names of the elements (and to impress your teachers!).

CHEMICAL FORMULA
(example:
NaCl)

This is used to help you learn the symbols of the elements. As you get further along in school, you will have to memorize the symbols. It will be helpful to know them.

SETTING UP
YOUR LAB

You should find a place to keep all of your materials for your chemistry experiments. A large box will be preferable. Talk to your parents about finding a good place to store the box. Keep in mind that many of the chemicals you will be using are dangerous. If you have younger children in your home, you will have to choose a storage spot for your box that will be safe from them.

The chemistry experiments in this book should be done on the kitchen table so that the sink and stove are easily accessible. Cover the table with newspapers before each experiment to protect the table. Change the papers between experiments. Some experiments will need to be done outside or in another area of your home. You may assume that any experiment can be done in the kitchen unless otherwise stated in the experiment.

In addition to the precautions listed above, it is a good idea to wear an apron to protect your clothes, and to wear safety goggles when using chemicals that might splash and injure your eyes.

Always wash and dry your equipment carefully after use. This is very important. Dirty equipment could cause reactions you don't want and give false results or a dangerous reaction. Always wash your hands after each experiment, and never put your fingers in your mouth or eyes while working on an experiment.

SUPPLIES YOU MAY NOT HAVE AT HOME AND WHERE TO FIND THEM

iron pills—drugstore, section near the vitamins

mucilage—stationery department of discount store, drugstore, or supermarket

cobalt chloride—hobby shop

Ex-Lax tablets—drugstore (laxative)

Alka-Seltzer tablets—drugstore (antacid)

red cabbage—supermarket (fresh vegetable area)

iodine—drugstore (first-aid section)

4–5 pieces of coal or brick—coal can be obtained from a coal dealer (look in the Yellow Pages)

laundry bluing—most stores no longer sell this in the laundry detergent section. You will have to order it by sending $3.00 to: Mrs. Stewart's Laundry Bluing, Luther Ford Products Co., 100 N. 7th Street, Minneapolis, MN 55403.

mothflakes—discount department store (housewares section)

chicken wire or fine wire screening—hardware store

simmer ring—discount department store (housewares section), or use a double boiler.

1 gallon glass jar with lid, or beaker with a wide mouth and suitable lid—the gallon jar can be obtained from an institution that uses large jars. Such places are: nursing homes, hospitals, cafeterias, and restaurants.

washing soda—supermarket (detergent section)

One summer day my friend Dan Hartmen and I were exploring near an abandoned house in the woods. Suddenly a white object sticking out of a hole in a tree trunk near us caught my eye.

"That's too high for us to reach," I said.

"Not if we climb the tree next to it with low branches," Dan replied.

"That's a good idea," I said, and began climbing the tree. I reached in, pulled out a sheet of paper, and handed it down to Dan.

"What a waste of time," Dan shouted as I jumped out of the tree.

"Why do you say that?" I asked.

"Take a look—it's blank," he answered.

"Maybe and maybe not. I have an idea. Let's go back to your house and borrow your mother's iron."

Dan and I used his mother's iron to bring out the secret writing on the paper. Not all secret writing is activated by using a hot iron. It depends on the material used to create the writing. In this case it worked. When we brought out the secret writing we found out it had been written by a boy to his friend. The message read:

> Dear Jim,
> Meet me at 2:00 on Tuesday at the old house. Bring your bike with you. I found a great path in the woods.
>
> > Billy

Various acetic liquids can be used to create secret writing. You can try cold tea, orange juice, lemon juice, or milk. Do they all dry to an invisible state? Do they all reappear as brown writing when a warm iron is applied? Which one works best?

I used lemon juice. It becomes invisible when it dries. The heat from the iron reacts with the acid in the lemon, and the secret message appears brown on the paper.

The following experiment will show in detail how to create and reveal hidden messages.

REVEALING HIDDEN MESSAGES

EQUIPMENT

pointed stick or artist's brush
1 tablespoon lemon juice (citric acid, CH_2COOH)
piece of paper
CAUTION electric iron

EXPERIMENT

Step 1. Dip the pointed stick or artist's brush in the lemon juice and write a secret message.

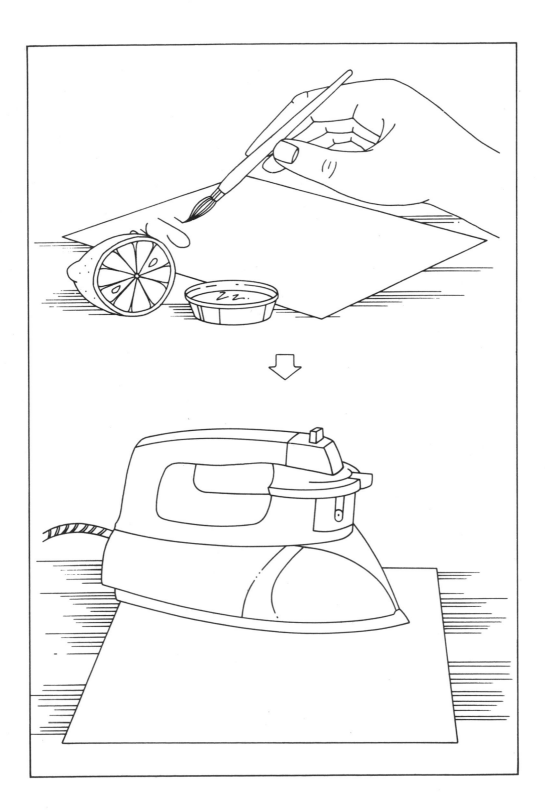

Step 2. Allow the message to dry. This may take several hours.

CAUTION Step 3. After the message has dried, go over the writing with a warm electric iron.

Have you ever used an iron before? Have an adult show you how to use one correctly.

2

It was 10:00 P.M. and I was getting ready to go to bed when the phone rang. It was my classmate, Eden.

She said, "Alan, I just realized I have a poster due for English tomorrow, and my only black felt-tip pen is dry. Does Captain Chemical have any suggestions?"

"Why don't you try the Black Ink Formula? You will have to wait until morning to use it, but you can do everything else tonight and get up early tomorrow to finish."

"Thanks a lot, Captain," she said. "You saved my grade."

Before I give you the formula Eden used, I'll explain how the experiment works.

The hot water dissolves the iron and tea. The reaction between the iron pills and the acid in the tea forms ink.

Mucilage can be used as a binding agent to make the ink thicker. What other things could you use to thicken the ink to the right consistency?

THE BLACK INK FORMULA

EQUIPMENT

4 iron pills (ferrous sulfate, $FeSO_4$)
$1/4$ cup warm tap water (H_2O)
1 saucepan
CAUTION 2 tablespoons boiling water (H_2O)
1 teabag (active ingredient: tannic acid, $C_{14}H_{10}O_9$)
1 jar and lid (approximately 8 oz./240 ml)
pointed stick or artist's brush
2 teaspoons mucilage

EXPERIMENT

Step 1. Soak the iron pills in $1/4$ cup warm water.
Step 2. Wait about 15 minutes for the colored coating on the pills to soak off.
CAUTION Step 3. Meanwhile, boil a small amount of water in the saucepan. Put 2 tablespoons of boiling water in the jar and add the teabag. Let sit 15 minutes.
Step 4. Drain the colored water from the iron pills.
Step 5. Remove the teabag from the jar.
Step 6. Add the iron to the tea.
Step 7. The iron pills will dissolve in the hot tea. Let it sit overnight.
Step 8. Pour a small amount of the ink in the lid of the jar. Using the stick or the brush, try writing your name with it.
Step 9. If the ink seems too thin, try adding 2 teaspoons mucilage to it as a binder.

Always have an adult with you if an experiment requires you to use the stove.

21 /

3

I began working on this book in the fifth grade in Bushy Park Elementary School.

After I had been working on it for about five months, my teacher, Mrs. Day, suggested I perform some simple experiments for the second graders at the school.

I chose three experiments for them to observe.

For the Rock Salt Crystal Experiment I needed a stove, so the teacher brought in a hotplate for me to use. I did that experiment first because the solution needed to cool before I could complete the experiment.

While the solution was cooling, I also performed the Magic Balloon Experiment and the Ice Cube Lift. I left the Rock Salt Crystal Experiment in the classroom for the students to observe daily for changes.

THE ROCK SALT
CRYSTAL EXPERIMENT

EQUIPMENT

1 jar (approximately 8 oz./240 ml)
water (H_2O)
1 saucepan
1 teaspoon salt (sodium chloride, NaCl)
1 mixing spoon
CAUTION stove
potholder
a piece of string about 6 in. (15 cm) long
1 paper clip
1 Popsicle stick

EXPERIMENT

Step 1. Fill the jar three-quarters full of water.

Step 2. Pour the water into the saucepan.

Step 3. Add 1 teaspoon of salt to the saucepan and stir until it is dissolved.

Step 4. Repeat step 3 until no more salt will dissolve. This may take a total of 12 or more teaspoons of salt.

CAUTION Step 5. When no more salt will dissolve, heat the saucepan on the stove. Do not boil the water.

Step 6. When you are sure the solution is hot (when you see bubbles just starting to appear), add 1 more teaspoon of salt and stir.

CAUTION Step 7. Remove the saucepan from the heat. Be sure to use a potholder. Allow to cool.

Step 8. After the solution has cooled, pour it into the jar.

Step 9. Tie the string around the middle of the Popsicle stick and tie the other end of the string to the paper clip (to keep it suspended).

Step 10. Suspend the string into the solution by balancing the stick across the top of the jar. Do not let the paper clip touch the bottom of the jar. If it does, wind it a turn or two around the stick.

Step 11. Put the jar someplace where it will not be disturbed and where it will be warm.

Step 12. Observe daily.

As the water evaporates, the salt returns to a solid state and attaches to the string.

There are two other experiments in this book involving crystals: The Mysterious Snow-Capped Mountain (page 64) and The Mystical Mothball Tree (page 69).

Always have an adult with you when the experiment requires you to use the stove. Always use a potholder.

THE MYSTERY OF
THE MAGIC BALLOON

EQUIPMENT

1 soft drink bottle (16 oz./480 ml)
1 tall container to hold the bottle (1 qt. deli container that held potato salad is perfect)
CAUTION hot water (H_2O)
1 balloon

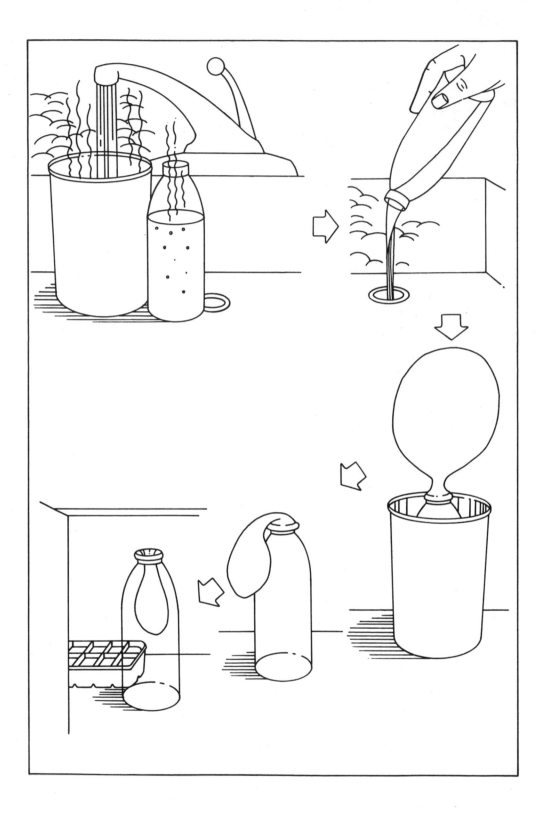

EXPERIMENT

Step 1. Fill the soft drink bottle with hot water.

CAUTION Step 2. Fill the tall container one-half to three-quarters full of hot water.

Step 3. When the bottle feels very warm, empty the water.

Step 4. Stretch the balloon over the mouth of the bottle.

Step 5. Put the bottle in the container of hot water until the balloon fills with air.

Step 6. Remove the bottle from the container.

Step 7. If you did not see a change occur within 45 seconds, return the bottle to the container.

Step 8. Put the bottle in the refrigerator or the freezer, leave the door open.

Step 9. Observe.

Warm air causes the balloon to expand. When the cool air surrounds the bottle it makes the balloon contract, pushing it into the bottle.

Be careful not to burn yourself when using hot water.

THE ICE CUBE LIFT

EQUIPMENT

1 jar (approximately 8 oz./240 ml)
water (H_2O)
1 ice cube
4-in. (10-cm) piece of string
salt (sodium chloride, NaCl)

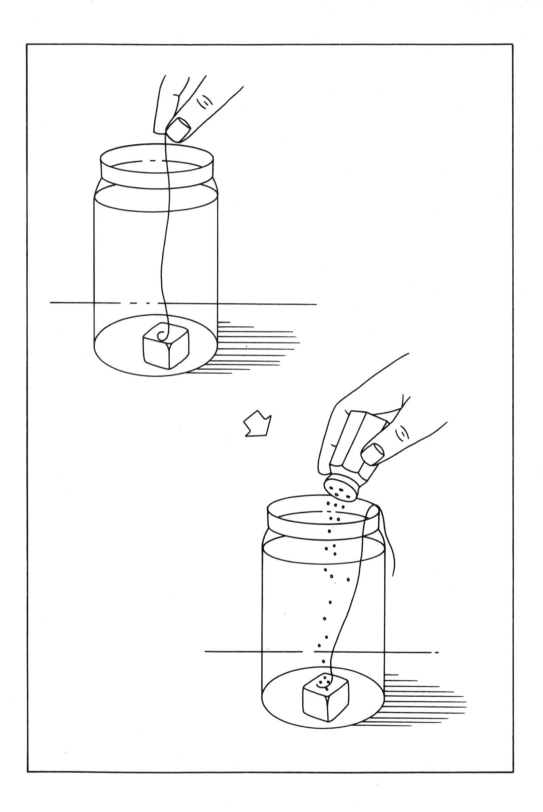

EXPERIMENT

Step 1. Fill jar with water.
Step 2. Drop in ice cube.
Step 3. Drop the end of the string onto the ice cube.
Step 4. Try to pick up the ice cube with the string.
Step 5. With the string on the ice cube sprinkle salt on the ice cube.
Step 6. Wait 45 seconds.
Step 7. Try to lift the ice cube again.

The freezing point of the ice is lowered by the salt. This makes a hole in the ice. Within 45 seconds the hole refreezes around the string so that the string is stuck in the ice. The melting ice gives off heat, and the ice cube will make the salt water refreeze. With the string stuck in the ice, it makes it possible to lift the ice cube out of the jar.

4

One evening at dinner my father said to me, "I received a letter today from your friend Thomas's father."

Thomas and his family were our next-door neighbors until last summer when they moved to Pennsylvania. His father had been offered the presidency of a small-town bank.

"What did he have to say?" I asked.

"His bank is having a problem," my dad said. "Someone there is altering checks written with felt-tip pens, changing 'eight' to 'eighty' and so on."

"Each manufacturer of felt-tip pens uses a different chemical formula. That makes each ink fade differently when exposed to water," I quickly replied. "Please, Dad, let's phone him right away. I think I can help."

"Okay, you can call after dinner," he said.

I wolfed down dessert and called. Thomas answered the phone. We talked for a few minutes, and then I asked for his dad. When he came to the phone, he asked me the same question he always asked.

"Have you blown up your basement yet?"

"Not exactly," I said. "My dad told me about your problem, and I need to ask you one question. Does your bank supply its employees with felt-tip pens?"

"No, we don't," he replied.

"Good," I said. "I have a possible solution for you. Have each employee write out the words sixty, seventy, eighty, and ninety, and the numbers 60, 70, 80, and 90 on an index card using their own felt-tip pen. Have them sign the card at the top. Collect all the cards and submerge them one by one in water, making sure you do not submerge the portion where the name is written. Then submerge one of the altered checks in the water also. Compare the way the ink faded on the altered part of the check with the index cards. If the ink on the card fades the same way as the ink faded on the check, then you will know who the counterfeiter is."

"That sounds like a chemical experiment I can handle," Mr. Hogan replied.

"And one that won't blow up your bank either," I said.

Later that week Thomas's father called to say, "Your experiment worked! The counterfeiter has been caught."

Each manufacturer uses a different chemical formula for the ink in felt-tip pens. This makes the ink fade differently. When you perform the experiment, you can easily see that the "ty" and extra zero were added with a different felt-tip pen.

THE CLUE IN THE
COUNTERFEIT CHECK

EQUIPMENT

1 index card
2 different felt-tip pens of the same color
jar (approximately 8 oz./240 ml)
tap water (H_2O)

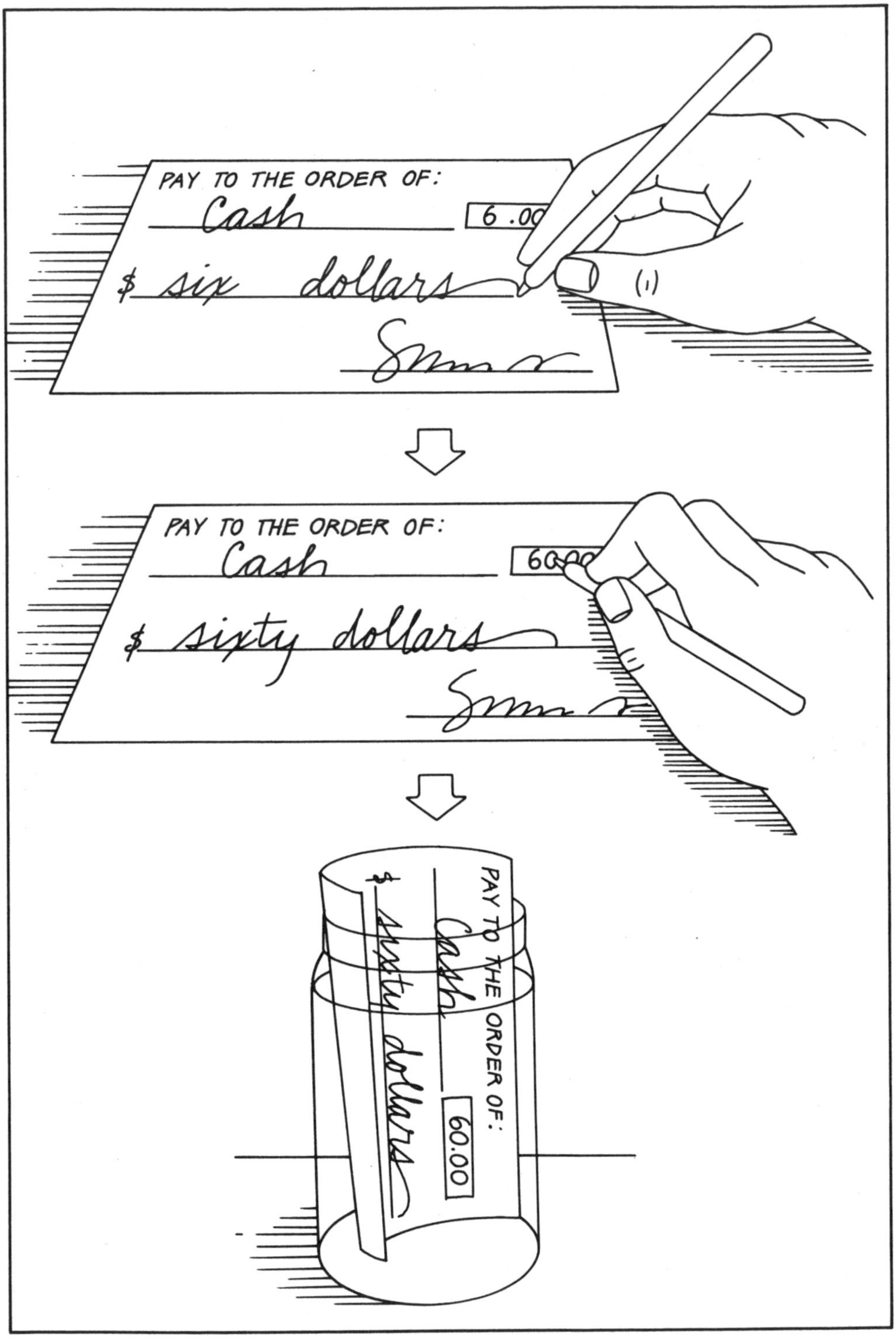
PAY TO THE ORDER OF:
Cash
6.00
$ six dollars
PAY TO THE ORDER OF:
Cash
60.00
$ sixty dollars
PAY TO THE ORDER OF:
Cash
60.00
$ sixty dollars

EXPERIMENT

Step 1. Write a "check" on an index card with one of the felt-tip pens. For the dollar amount choose an amount between six and nine, spelled out. These amounts can be easily changed (by adding "ty").

Step 2. After you have written the check for six, seven, eight, or nine dollars, add "ty" to the written number and a zero to the numeral with the other felt-tip pen.

Step 3. Allow the ink to dry.

Step 4. Fill the jar with water.

Step 5. Put the check in the water.

Step 6. Observe the check as you withdraw it from the water.

5

I was at my friend's house. His father had a habit of drinking Alka-Seltzer continuously. He said to me, "A good mystery to solve would be to find out a good use for this Alka-Seltzer besides my father drinking it."

So we spent part of the day experimenting with Alka-Seltzer. We tried macaroni, unsalted peanuts, mothballs, salted peanuts, bits of cheese, and raisins.

Some of them worked, but the best reaction was obtained by using raisins.

The Alka-Seltzer releases carbon dioxide gas. The gas collects on the raisins as little bubbles. Because the gas is lighter than the water, the raisins rise to the surface. On the surface the gas bubbles leave the raisins, causing them to sink to the bottom again. This gives the impression that the raisins are performing mysterious acrobatic feats.

Try this experiment and see if you can get some raisins to perform for you.

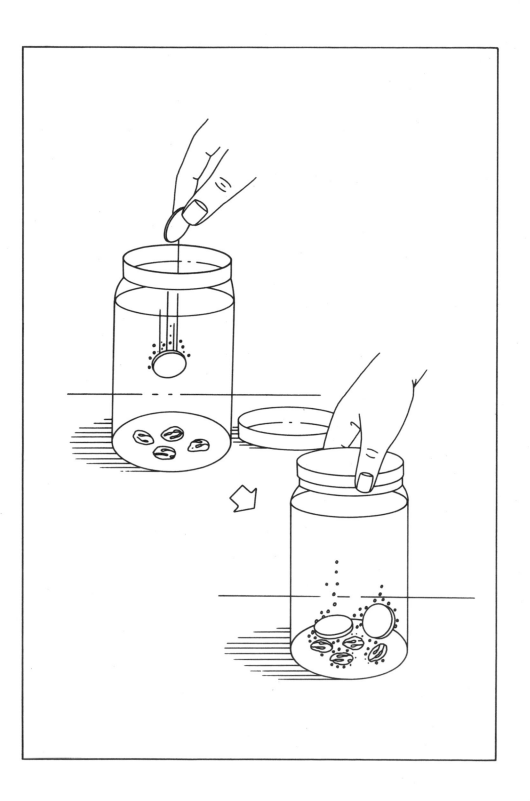

THE SECRET OF
THE ACROBATIC RAISINS

EQUIPMENT

small jar with lid (approximately 8 oz./240 ml)
tap water (H_2O)
4–5 raisins
2 Alka-Seltzer tablets

EXPERIMENT

Step 1. Fill jar three-quarters full with tap water.
Step 2. Drop 4–5 raisins in jar.
Step 3. Drop 2 Alka-Seltzer tablets in jar.
Step 4. Quickly put lid on jar.

Note: Keeping the lid on the jar prevents the carbon dioxide (CO_2) from escaping. This results in a more impressive and longer lasting experiment.

6

It was the first weekend of the new school year. I thought I could lie back and relax, but my dream suddenly faded. Early Saturday morning I received a phone call from Mrs. Jones, my friend Tom's mother. "As you know, Alan," she said, "for several years I have been selling homemade pies, cakes, and cookies at the Farmer's Market. I recently purchased a recipe for making gumdrops from a company that was going out of business. I have no way of getting in touch with them again. I've tried the recipe several times, and I just can't get it to work."

"What seems to be the problem?" I asked.

"They don't hold together," she replied. "Can you detect what might be wrong with the recipe? A recipe isn't much different from a chemical formula."

"What do you use to make them?" I asked.

"I use water, food coloring, and sugar."

"No gelatin?" I interrupted.

"No, why?" came the answer.

"No wonder the company went out of business! You don't have any collagen in the product," I said.

"What is collagen, and where can I buy it?" she wanted to know.

"You can't buy it," I replied, "but you can get it by using gelatin," I said.

"Please tell me exactly what to do," she said.

Gelatin is a breakdown product of collagen, a protein found in bones, ligaments, and tendons. It holds us together. The gelatin swells by holding the water, causing a gumdrop to form. I explained this to Mrs. Jones and then gave her the instructions to follow. She calls it a recipe; I call it a chemical experiment.

THE CASE OF THE DISAPPOINTING GUMDROPS

EQUIPMENT

1 small pack of unflavored gelatin
small cup
medicine dropper
tap water (H_2O)
lemon extract
fork

EXPERIMENT

Step 1. Pour entire pack of unflavored gelatin into cup.
Step 2. Put one drop of water into gelatin.
Step 3. Wait until it is absorbed.
Step 4. Repeat steps 2 and 3 fifteen more times.
Step 5. Add 3 drops of lemon extract.
Step 6. With a fork, scoop out the jellied ball.
Step 7. Taste it. Good, isn't it?

7

It was a cold, windy, rainy day. What a perfect day to work in my chemistry lab without interruptions.

I had only been working about an hour, when there was a loud knock at the door. I opened the door to find a very wet man with a huge umbrella.

He said, "I am Mr. Lee from the White Rice Palace Restaurant. I am in desperate need of your services."

"You must be desperate to come out on a day like this," I said. "Come in and sit down. Would you like a hot cup of coffee? I can get my mom to make it for you."

"I would prefer tea if you have it," he said.

As he drank his tea, and I drank my hot chocolate, he told me his story.

He had gone to his restaurant shortly after noon to begin preparing for dinner. The evening before he had cooked a huge amount of rice to be used in preparing fried rice for today's dinner. It was his habit to do this just before closing time. Preparing the rice the night before gave him extra time the following afternoon to cook the other foods he needed to complete his menu.

When he took the rice out of the refrigerator today it was *blue*! Mr. Lee was beside himself. He could start over again, but what if that batch also turned blue? Since Mr. Lee was on such a tight time schedule, I was glad that I knew exactly what had happened.

"It is very obvious to me what has happened," I said. "After you finished cooking the rice, you didn't put it in the refrigerator yourself, did you, Mr. Lee?"

"No, I didn't. How did you know that?" he asked.

"It is very obvious that someone who works for you accidentally spilled iodine over the rice," I said. "Look for someone working for you with a cut on their hand, and you will find the person who spilled iodine over the rice and was afraid to tell you."

"But iodine is brown, not blue," countered Mr. Lee.

"Oh, you are right," I said. "But iodine is an indicator, a substance that indicates a chemical change, especially by changing color. Starch contains carbon, hydrogen, and oxygen. When the elements in starch react with iodine it turns blue. In this case the rice is the starch. Come into my lab, and I will show you."

Mr. Lee was amazed when I did the experiment for him. In return for solving the mystery of the blue rice, he invited our whole family to dinner at his restaurant. What a delicious meal it was, accompanied by heaping mounds of fluffy *white* rice.

This is the experiment I did for Mr. Lee. After you do it, you might want to try detecting the presence of starch in other foods.

THE MYSTERIOUS CHAMELEON RICE

EQUIPMENT

2 cups water (H_2O)
saucepan (3 cup/720 ml)

stove
1 teaspoon rice
strainer
plastic food storage container (1 qt. size)
plate
5 drops iodine (I)

EXPERIMENT

Step 1. Place 2 cups of water in the saucepan.
Step 2. Heat it on the stove until it boils.
Step 3. Add 1 teaspoon rice and lower heat to a slow boil for 20 minutes.
Step 4. Strain the water off the rice into the plastic food storage container.
Step 5. Put the rice on the plate and add 1–2 teaspoons of rice water.
Step 6. Mash the rice with the back of the teaspoon until it loses its shape.
Step 7. Add about 5 drops iodine to the mound of rice.

I was working on some experiments with cooking oil, when I happened to perform an experiment that produced an eerie eye effect. There is an old saying—oil and water do not mix. This experiment proves that.

THE EERIE EYE
EFFECT EXPERIMENT

EQUIPMENT

small clear medicine bottle
rubbing alcohol ($CH_3CHOHCH_3$)
water (H_2O)

medicine dropper
cooking oil
food coloring

EXPERIMENT

Step 1. Pour rubbing alcohol into the bottle until it is about two-thirds full.
Step 2. Add one-third water.
Step 3. With the medicine dropper, drop cooking oil into the liquid until there is a bubble almost as big as the mouth of the bottle floating on top.
Step 4. Add one drop of food coloring (any color but yellow) into the center of the bubble.
Step 5. Observe.

To make the oil form a bubble, it is necessary to mix a liquid of a low density with a heavier one. (Density is the measurement of how closely the particles of a substance are packed together.) The density of water is greater than the density of the alcohol.

Because oil and water do not mix, the water-based food coloring gets trapped in the oil. It takes a little time for the drop of suspended food coloring to penetrate through the depth of the oil bubble and escape to the other side. Try watching the experiment looking down into the bottle from the top. Repeat the experiment and watch it from the side of the bottle.

9

Not long after the incident of the Mysterious Chameleon Rice, I was telling my friend, Ryan LaFon, about the experience. My story seemed to interest him so much that he decided to find out more about indicators. He asked me to suggest some experiments he could try using indicators. There are many interesting indicators used to detect the presence of different kinds of substances. One experiment I told Ryan about was the Mysterious Changeable Weatherman. I explained to Ryan that I had performed this experiment last June, several days before our annual class picnic. I had been watching the weather reports on television for several days. On each channel the weatherman gave a different forecast. I decided to predict the weather for the day of the picnic myself. I predicted sunny weather, and it turned out to be a perfect day. This is how I did it.

I also suggested the Secret of the Rapidly Ripening Apples and the Red Cabbage Caper.

THE MYSTERIOUS
CHANGEABLE WEATHERMAN

EQUIPMENT

scissors
coffee filters
2 Popsicle sticks
string about 6 in. (15 cm) long
cobalt chloride ($CoCl_2$)
jar (approximately 8 oz./240 ml)
saucepan (optional)
water (H_2O)

CAUTION stove (optional)

EXPERIMENT

Step 1. Cut the coffee filter in half and wrap each half around a Popsicle stick, leaving a little extra on each end of the stick. (These will be hands and feet.)

Step 2. Cross the two sticks and tie them perpendicular to each other at the cross with the string. You should have a scarecrow-like figure. You can wrap a little extra coffee filter at the top for a head.

Step 3. Dip each arm and leg into the bottle of cobalt chloride. It's all right if the solution does not reach all of the way up the arms and legs. It will spread by absorption.

Step 4. Allow the "weatherman" to dry by resting it across the mouth of the jar.

Step 5. Observe him several times a day for a few days.

If you can't wait that long, place him near the stove and heat a saucepan of water. Now observe your weatherman. Always have an adult with you when you use the stove.

49 /

Cobalt chloride is another example of an indicator. This indicator reacts to moisture in the air. Cobalt chloride liquid is pink. When the humidity or water in the air increases, the weatherman will turn blue, because the cobalt chloride bonds with the water. That means he can predict rain.

THE SECRET OF THE RAPIDLY RIPENING APPLES

EQUIPMENT

apron
safety goggles
1 sheet of paper
pencil
CAUTION Ex-Lax tablet
1 cup
CAUTION 1 tablespoon isopropyl alcohol ($CH_3CHOHCH$)
CAUTION household ammonia (ammonium hydroxide, NH_4OH)
artist's brush

EXPERIMENT

Step 1. Put on apron and goggles.
Step 2. Draw a picture of a tree as big as the paper.
Step 3. Place your spread-out hand on the paper and at each fingertip draw an apple.
Step 4. Crush the Ex-Lax tablet in the cup with the tablespoon.
Step 5. Mix the Ex-Lax tablet with 1 tablespoon isopropyl alcohol.
Step 6. Paint the apples on the tree with the mixture in Step 4. This is liquid phenolphthalein ($C_{20}H_{14}O_4$).
Step 7. Pour the ammonia into the lid of the ammonia bottle.

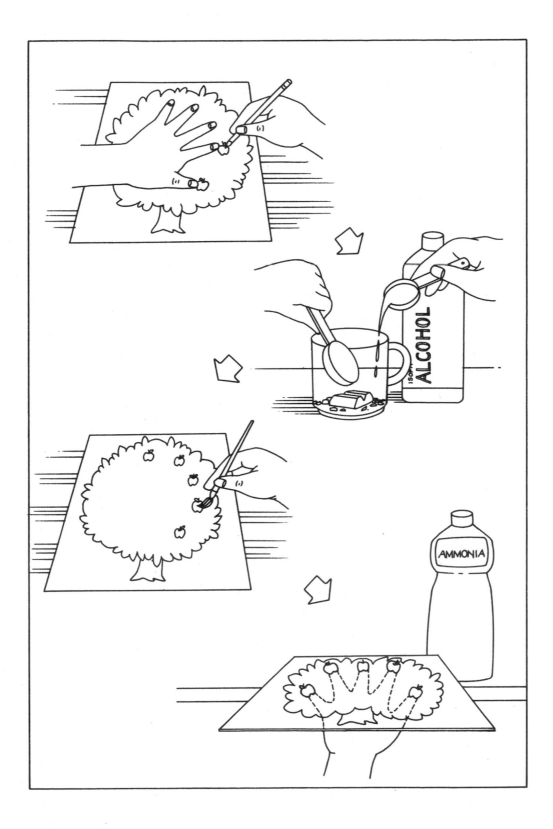

Step 8. Dip your fingertips in the household ammonia and spread your fingers against the *back* of the picture, behind each apple, while observing the picture.

The apples on the tree will suddenly and mysteriously ripen and turn red. Phenolphthalein is the active ingredient in Ex-Lax. The alcohol is added to get it into solution. The indicator phenolphthalein turns red in the presence of an alkali solution. It indicates that household ammonia is an alkali solution.

Ex-Lax tablets are medicine. They look like chocolate candy and even one tablet can be very dangerous for a small child. Have your parents keep them in a safe place for you.

Isopropyl alcohol can burn your eyes. Be careful not to splash when pouring it. Wash your hands after using it. Put this away immediately. A small child could be poisoned by drinking it.

Household ammonia is a very strong reacting liquid. Follow the same rules as with alcohol. In addition, household ammonia emits a strong, offensive, and dangerous odor. Do not leave the bottle open for long and do not sniff the fumes. Be sure to wash your hands well immediately after performing this experiment. Take additional safety precautions by wearing safety goggles and an apron.

THE RED CABBAGE CAPER

EQUIPMENT

apron
goggles

red cabbage
saucepan (3 cup/720 ml)
water (H_2O)

CAUTION stove
jar
teaspoon
vinegar (acetic acid, CH_3COOH)
household ammonia (ammonium hydroxide, NH_4OH)

EXPERIMENT

Step 1. Put on apron and goggles.

Step 2. Put a handful of red cabbage leaves in the saucepan and cover with water.

CAUTION Step 3. Cook on the stove until the cabbage has lost all of its color, about 20 minutes.

CAUTION Step 4. Allow the juice to cool.

Step 5. Pour the juice into the jar and observe its color.

Step 6. Add 10 teaspoons (approximately) of vinegar.

Step 7. Add 12 teaspoons of household ammonia.

Red cabbage and many purple flowers contain a substance that gives them their color and that has the added property of acting as an indicator. The red cabbage juice will be purple initially. Red cabbage juice is an indicator that changes color when it comes in contact with an acid or a base. The vinegar, which is an acid, turns the red cabbage juice more red. The household ammonia, which is a base, turns the solution green.

It is important to have an adult with you when you use the stove.

Do not pour the juice into the jar while it is still hot. If the juice is hot it could break the jar and send out flying glass.

Household ammonia can burn your eyes. Be careful not to splash when pouring it. Wash your hands after use so that if you got any on your hands, you won't rub it in your eyes later. This is a very dangerous liquid, keep it away from any small children.

10

On my way to English class my friend, Jim, approached me in the hall. He said to me, "Alan, I have another mystery for you. A couple of days ago, I was using steel wool to clean up some pots and pans from a camping trip. Last night when I went back to finish, the steel wool had turned brown. I didn't know whether to use it or not after that. Will it still work? Will it leave brown spots on the pans?"

"Steel wool is made from iron," I said. "The iron takes on oxygen from water (oxidizes). When iron oxidizes it rusts. The reddish-brown rust on the steel wool is called ferric oxide. Your steel wool got damp in some way. It will still do the job for you.

"There is an experiment you can do that will demonstrate the mystery of rust formation at different rates. Steel wool will oxidize faster when bleach is added to the water, because the chlorine in the bleach is very attracted to the hydrogen in the water. When it combines with the hydrogen, the oxygen is released. If you mix water, bleach, and vinegar, additional oxygen is released from the vinegar. With oxygen being released from the water, the bleach, and the vinegar the result is even more rapid oxidation or rusting."

Here is the experiment that I told Jim about.

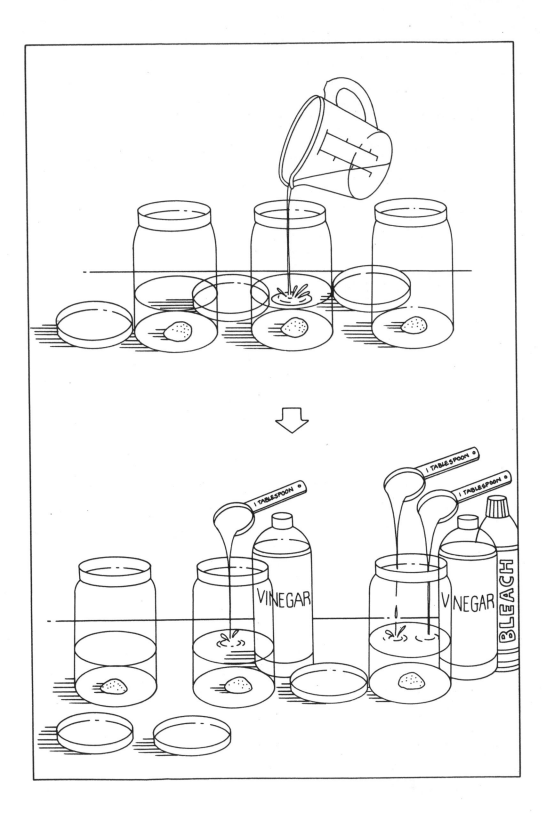

THE STEEL WOOL DISGUISE

EQUIPMENT

apron

goggles

3 small balls of steel wool (use steel wool without soap, and pull one piece apart to make 3 balls)

3 jars with lids (approximately 8 oz./240 ml)

water (H_2O)

1 tablespoon vinegar (acetic acid, CH_3COOH)

CAUTION 1 tablespoon bleach (sodium hypochlorite, $NaClO$)

EXPERIMENT

Step 1. Put on apron and safety goggles.

Step 2. Put a small ball of steel wool in each jar.

Step 3. Cover the steel wool with water.

Step 4. To the second jar add 1 tablespoon vinegar.

CAUTION Step 5. To the third jar add the same amount of vinegar and 1 tablespoon bleach.

Step 6. Within 15 to 30 minutes you should notice a change.

Step 7. Record the change and the jar in which it occurred.

Step 8. Observe the jars again after a few hours and record your observations.

Step 9. Observe the jars for the last time after 24 hours and record your observations.

Bleach is a dangerous liquid. It will permanently remove the color from fabric. Don't spill any on your clothes or carpet. It is best to wear an apron. Be very careful not to splash any in your eyes. It could damage your eyes permanently. To be safe, wear goggles. Be sure to wash your hands after using it.

11

On the day after Thanksgiving, my younger cousin, Mark, called me sounding very upset.

"Alan, I am so mad, because I can't go to a magic show this afternoon," Mark complained.

"Why can't you go?" I asked.

"I have chickenpox," he replied. "The poster advertised a magic trick about a phantom in a bottle. I was really looking forward to seeing that."

"I don't know how the magician was going to bring about a phantom in a bottle, but I know how to make a mysterious chemical phantom appear in a bottle."

"Will you come over and show me?" he asked.

"I'll go ask my mom when I can come," I answered.

My mom let me go, because I had already had chickenpox.

The explanation for this experiment is that the hot water, just like hot air, expands and rises, because it is lighter, while the cold water stays at the bottom. This is why colored water is used—so that we can see the hot water rise.

58 /

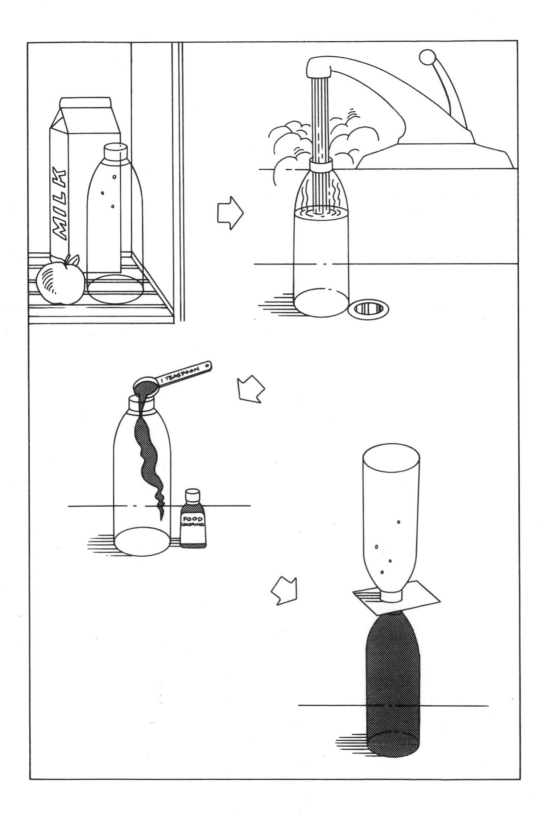

THE PHANTOM
IN THE BOTTLE

EQUIPMENT

2 clear plastic soft-drink bottles (16 oz./480 ml)
cold water (H_2O)
CAUTION hot water (H_2O)
2 teaspoons dark food coloring
1 index card

EXPERIMENT

Step 1. Fill one bottle with cold water and place it in the refrigerator.
CAUTION Step 2. Fill the other bottle with hot water.
Step 3. Add 2 teaspoons food coloring to the bottle of hot water.
Step 4. Remove the bottle from the refrigerator and place the index card over the opening.
Step 5. Invert the cold bottle on top of the hot bottle. Be sure to keep the index card between the two bottles.
Step 6. Slowly and carefully slide the index card out from between the bottles.

The experiment should work with hot tap water. You still must be careful not to get burned. THE BEST PLACE TO DO THIS EXPERIMENT IS IN THE KITCHEN SINK!

12

On the morning of April 1 I heard a shriek from the kitchen. I ran in to see what had happened. I noticed the celery sitting on the kitchen table was a bright red!

My mom asked me, "Alan, did you have anything to do with this?"

I said, "No," laughing.

"What do you think could have happened?" she asked.

I told her that it reminded me of the Stalking the Colored Celery Stalk experiment.

My father walked in and said, "I see you found my April Fools' joke."

Plants get their food and water through hollow tubes in their stems. This is called capillary action. Water is cohesive (it sticks to itself) and also very adhesive (it sticks to other things). Because of these two properties it is able to defy gravity. Along with the capillary action, these properties make the experiment produce such amazing and mysterious results.

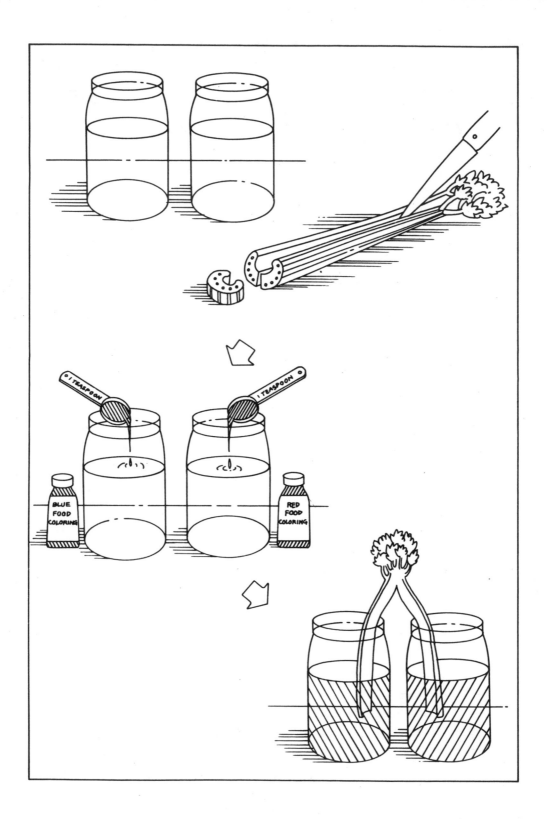

STALKING THE
COLORED CELERY STALK

EQUIPMENT

2 jars (approximately 8 oz./240 ml)
water (H_2O)
knife
1 stalk of celery with leaves
1 teaspoon red food coloring
1 teaspoon blue food coloring

EXPERIMENT

Step 1. Fill the jars halfway with water.
Step 2. Cut a ½ in. (1–2 cm) piece off the bottom of the celery.
Step 3. Cut the celery stalk lengthwise from 1 in. (2–3 cm) below the leaves to the bottom.
Step 4. Put 1 teaspoon red food coloring in one jar, and 1 teaspoon blue food coloring in the other jar of water.
Step 5. Put one section of the celery stalk in one jar, and the other section in the other jar.
Step 6. Allow the jars to sit overnight.
Step 7. Observe the next morning.

13

I heard someone frantically calling my name as I entered the school cafeteria line one lunch time. Turning I saw my friend, Greg, hurrying towards me.

"Alan, I have a problem. Mrs. Kelly has assigned me the job of providing decorations for the county science-fair banquet. She doesn't want flowers on the tables. She wants something original that will convey the theme of science projects. I thought about using the science-fair entries, but they all have to remain on one table for judging. I just haven't got a clue as to what to do," he said.

"I have a project that will be on display that night too," I replied. "Actually, I can think of two other experiments that would work well as table centerpieces," I answered.

"That's great," he said, "tell me about them. Are they easy to do?"

"They are both experiments that deal with crystalization," I replied. "The Mystical Mothball Tree experiment is a little difficult to do only because it takes time to find the supplies. But, I can lend you those. It gives a very impressive result. Why not use that for the speakers' table? The other experiment, the Mysterious Snow-Capped Mountain, is fast and easy to prepare, but you have to do it about a week and a half before the banquet. By the time the banquet rolls around, it will be ready."

The coal or brick in the Mysterious Snow-Capped Mountain experiment is porous, and the solution poured into the bowl is absorbed by the coal or brick. If the coal or brick were not porous, the experiment could not be performed. The salt reacts with the household ammonia, forming ammonium chloride. When the solution that has reached the top of the coal or brick by capillary action evaporates into the air, the ammonium chloride that remains crystalizes. The laundry bluing enhances the reaction. The process continues for weeks.

In the Mystical Mothball Tree experiment the heating of the mothflakes causes them to liquify and vaporize. Then they condense in the cool part of the jar as crystals.

Now it is your turn to try to make "snow"!

THE MYSTERIOUS
SNOW-CAPPED MOUNTAIN

EQUIPMENT

4–5 pieces of brick or coal
hammer (if you use the brick)
goggles
apron

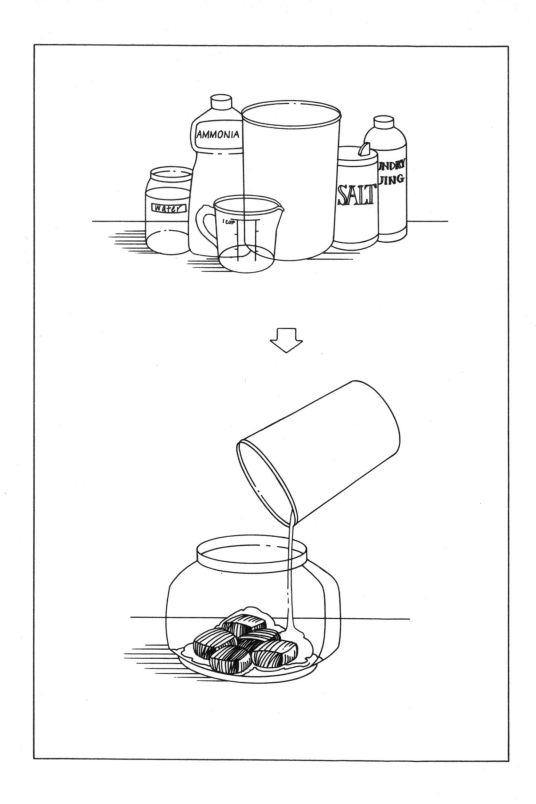

fishbowl or casserole dish
quart-size plastic container
large spoon
$3/4$ cup each of:

CAUTION laundry bluing (see p. 14)
water (H_2O)
CAUTION household ammonia (ammonium hydroxide, NH_4OH)
salt (sodium chloride, NaCl)

EXPERIMENT

Step 1. (Do this step if you use brick instead of coal.) Go out of doors. Put goggles on to protect your eyes. With a hammer smash the brick into 2–3-in. (5–8 cm) pieces.

Step 2. Put on apron.

Step 3. Put 4–5 pieces of brick or coal into the bowl. Put a couple of pieces on top of each other to raise the height of the mountain.

CAUTION Step 4. Mix the laundry bluing, water, household ammonia, and salt in the quart-size plastic container or jar and stir with the large spoon.

Step 5. Pour this mixture into the bowl, but not over the coal or the bricks.

Step 6. If all of the salt does not dissolve, use the spoon to scrape it out of the container into the bowl.

Step 7. Wait a couple of days—observing daily.

Laundry bluing will permanently stain anything it touches. Be sure to pad table top with newspapers. Be careful not to splash it onto anything. It is best to protect your clothing with an apron.

Household ammonia is very poisonous. Be very careful when stirring or pouring, so that you don't splash any in your eyes. It is best to wear goggles. Be sure to wash your hands after use. Do not deliberately try to inhale the odor. The fumes can be harmful to your nose and lungs.

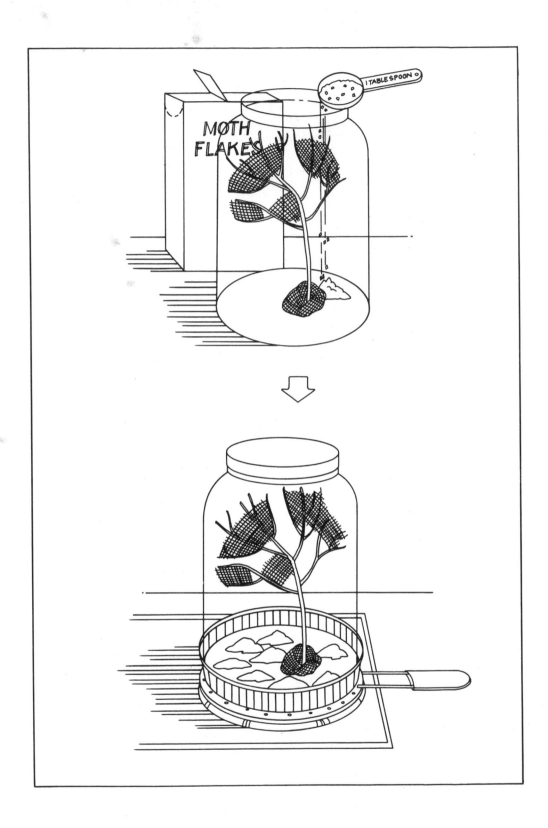

THE MYSTICAL
MOTHBALL TREE

Note: This is an easy experiment to do once you find the equipment. It is also a very beautiful experiment. It is well worth taking the time to get the proper equipment.

EQUIPMENT

tree twig with several little branches about 4–5 in. (10–12 cm).
piece of chicken wire or fine wire screening material about 6 × 12
    in. (15 × 30 cm)
wire cutter
CAUTION 8 tablespoons of mothflakes
CAUTION stove
    pie plate or cake pan
    1 gallon glass jar with lid, or
    a beaker with a wide mouth and a suitable lid*
    simmer ring**

*(If you can get a heat-resistant glass jar or beaker, that would be best, because it will have to be heated. Pyrex is an example of a heat-resistant container.) The container I used was not heat-resistant and it worked well. But, if you choose to do this, you must be aware that it could shatter while being heated, and protect yourself. The way to do this is to wear goggles to protect your eyes and to stand as far back from the stove as possible. A glass jar this size is difficult to find. They are called institutional jars and are used by hospitals, nursing homes, cafeterias, and restaurants. The difficulty is that many of the glass jars that food like mustard and pickles, etc., used to come in have been replaced by plastic jars. So it may take a while for you to find a glass one. If you know of a store that sells large pickled onions, you might be able to get a gallon glass jar there.

**This is a flat, metal, pan-type object with a frying pan handle. It is used on the stove with a saucepan instead of using a double boiler. They can be purchased from a mail order catalog or in the house-wares department of a discount department store. If you can't get one of these, get the adult who helps you with this experiment to show you how to make the pie plate or cake pan suspend over a saucepan that is just a little smaller than the plate or cake pan. The saucepan should be half full of water if you use this method.

EXPERIMENT

Step 1. Turn the twig upright so that it resembles a tree and cut wire or screening so that it will fit into the jar. Cut small pieces of wire, fitting it on the branches of the twig stretching from one branch to another. With the remainder make a ball and insert the base of the twig into it, manipulating it until it will act as a stand holding the tree upright.

Step 2. Put the tree into the jar.

CAUTION Step 3. Put the mothflakes into the bottom of the jar.

Step 4. Put the simmer ring on the stove burner.

Step 5. Put the pie plate or cake pan on the simmer ring.

Step 6. Put the jar in the pie plate or cake pan.

CAUTION Step 7. Place the lid on the jar. DO NOT SCREW THE LID IN PLACE. JUST SET IT ON THE TOP. Fumes come up as the jar is heated. The lid is put on to keep the hazardous fumes from escaping into the room and to keep the vapor inside the jar so that it can do its job. If the lid is screwed on, too much heat will be created in the jar and it will shatter.

CAUTION Step 8. Heat the jar.

Step 9. At some point you will begin to feel that the experiment is no longer advancing. When this happens, turn off the stove and lift the lid with a potholder. Let a little cool air from the room enter the jar and then recover. Wait about 5 minutes and repeat. Do this 4–5 times. Let the jar sit for a couple of hours. Reheat it again to get more of a reaction.

Mothflakes are very poisonous. Be sure to wash your hands after use. To keep the fumes of the mothflakes or the benzoic acid from irritating you, it is best to open the windows and turn on the exhaust fan over the stove if you have one.

Always have an adult with you when using the stove in any of these experiments.

Note: This experiment can also be done using benzoic acid ($C_7H_6O_2$), instead of the mothflakes. It can be purchased in a hobby shop that sells chemistry supplies. It gives a better result and only 3 tablespoons of the chemical is needed. A small jar of it can be purchased for about 95¢ and contains just about 3 tablespoons. The two drawbacks are that it is difficult to find a store that sells chemicals and the fumes are stronger and more irritating than the mothflakes.

Barett was a new friend I met in school this past year. He invited me to his house one Saturday. As luck would have it that was the first time it had rained in months. His little sister was very bored that day and kept hanging around us. Nothing seemed to interest her except what we were doing.

Finally I said to her, "How would you like to spend the afternoon making some chemical peacocks?" This sounded to her like something only big kids could do, and so really interested her.

I showed her how to do the experiment. After she did it, I suggested she remove the filter from the pan, attach pipe cleaners for legs, and glue on a head made from balled-up paper. She became very involved in the project. It kept her occupied for the rest of the afternoon, and Barett and I enjoyed an uninterrupted day together after that.

This type of experiment is known as chromatography. Chromatography is a method of testing a liquid mixture of a dye to discover what is in the mixture. The water is absorbed by the porous coffee

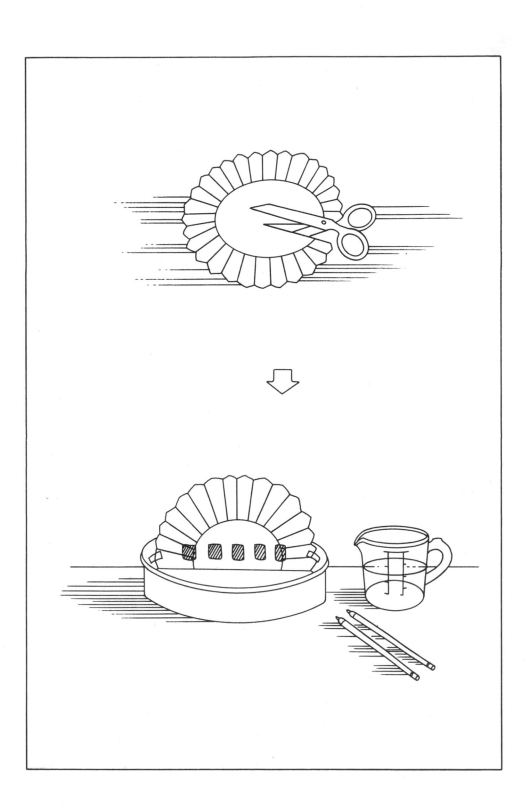

filter. The color of ink in each felt-tip pen is actually a combination of colors of different molecular weights. (Molecular weight is the weight of a molecule of a substance in relation to the weight of a single hydrogen atom.) When each colored ink comes in contact with the water, the various dyes in that color spread out at a different rate because of the different molecular weights in each dye.

THE KEY TO
THE PSEUDO PEACOCK

EQUIPMENT

coffee filter
scissors
several different-colored felt-tip pens
tape
cake pan
jar
water (H_2O)

EXPERIMENT

Step 1. Cut the coffee filter in half.
Step 2. About ¾ in. (2 cm) up from the cut edge, make several postage-stamp-size colored squares with the felt-tip pens.
Step 3. Tape the filter into the cake pan so that it stands up with the flat edge against the bottom of the cake pan.
Step 4. Add a small amount of water from the jar to the cake pan so that the bottom edge of the filter just begins to get wet.
Step 5. Observe.

15

My friend Jim always stops me between classes to get me to explain scientific phenomena to him. Last time he stopped me, he wanted to know why some things that he would have expected to sink in water, such as a piece of plastic, actually floated.

I told him that whether something is going to sink or float is dependent on surface tension as well as weight.

Water has a thin film across the top of it called surface tension. The film is invisible and is created by the molecules being packed together on the surface. Soaps and detergents break the surface tension. I advised Jim to try the following two experiments.

In the Secret of the Speeding Boat, the detergent breaks the surface tension behind the boat. The surface tension on the front and sides of the boat still pulls on the boat. With no resistance behind the boat it is pulled forward.

In the Secret of the Exploding Colors, rapid movement occurs in the water when the surface tension is broken. The colors swirl around in the liquid.

THE SECRET OF
THE SPEEDING BOAT

EQUIPMENT

bath tub
index card
scissors
liquid detergent
water (H_2O)

(If you live in an area that has hard water or if you have well water, you will also need a water softener such as washing soda—sodium carbonate, Na_2CO_3—to make the experiment work. Add about $\frac{1}{3}$ cup of washing soda to the bath water.)

EXPERIMENT

Step 1. Fill the tub with a couple of inches (5–6 cm) of water.
Step 2. Cut a boat from the index card in the shape shown in the illustration.
Step 3. After the water has been turned off, wait for it to get still and then put the boat at one end of the tub.
Step 4. Drop a drop of liquid detergent behind the boat.

Hard water does not make soap suds easily. It is the result of the water flowing over rocks containing minerals. The minerals in the water prevent the soap from making many suds by adhering to the soap.

   Water in large cities goes to a filtration plant where many chemicals are added for various reasons. Some of those chemicals "soften" the water. When washing soda is added to water, it reacts with the calcium salts forming calcium carbonate and sodium salts. This exchange also results in softening of the water.

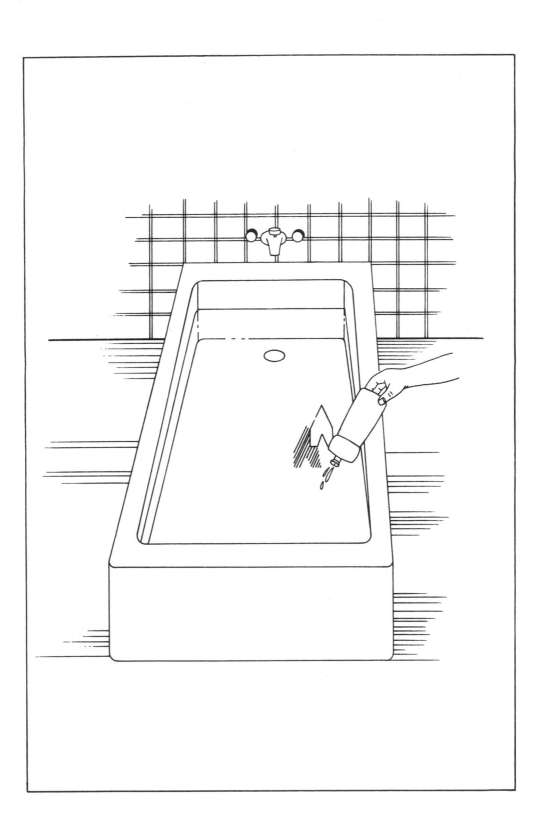

THE SECRET OF
THE EXPLODING COLORS

EQUIPMENT

small bowl
water (H_2O)
medicine dropper
food coloring
liquid detergent

EXPERIMENT

Step 1. Put 1 in. (2–3 cm) of water in the bowl.
Step 2. Wait for the water to get still.
Step 3. Drop one drop of food coloring at the edge of the bowl.
Step 4. Using at least one more color, and possibly as many as three more, drop one drop of each color at different spots around the bowl.
Step 5. Pour a few drops of liquid detergent down the side of the bowl.

16

After Dan and I exposed the secret message that we found in the tree at the abandoned house, we tried writing some secret messages.

Then I remembered that messages could be copied by using turpentine. Unfortunately, it cannot be used to replace duplicating machines because the copy comes out backwards!

But for Dan and me that could work to our advantage. We realized that we could communicate that way, and because the message was backwards, it was like using a code or secret writing. All we had to do to read the secret message was to hold it up to a mirror!

The addition of soap to the solution keeps the water and turpentine from separating. This kind of solution is called an emulsion. An emulsion is a mixture of one liquid suspended in another liquid by a substance that keeps them from separating. The ink on the comic strip is dissolved by the turpentine (turpentine is a solvent), and it comes off onto the typing paper.

Try the next experiment and you will be as amazed as we were with the results.

THE COMIC STRIP RUBOUT

EQUIPMENT

sheet of plastic 12 × 12 in. (30 × 30 cm) or bigger
2 sheets of typing paper
comic strip from newspaper (black and white or color)
jar with lid
turpentine
water (H_2O)
small piece of soap
paintbrush
spoon

EXPERIMENT

Step 1. Place the piece of plastic on a flat surface, put 1 piece of typing paper on top of the plastic, put the comic strip you would like to copy facedown on top of the typing paper.

CAUTION Step 2. Fill the jar lid one-half full of turpentine; pour it into the jar.

Step 3. Fill the lid with water two times and pour it into the jar.

Step 4. Observe the solution. The two liquids will not mix because of the large difference in their specific gravities.

Step 5. Add a small piece of soap to the mixture and shake the jar vigorously with the lid on the jar. If the liquids have not mixed together add more soap.

CAUTION Step 6. "Paint" the solution onto the comic strip with the paintbrush. Be sure to saturate the newspaper.

Step 7. Quickly place the second sheet of typing paper on top of the wet comic strip and rub over it with the back of a spoon.

Step 8. After you have gone over the entire section you want to copy, remove the top sheet of typing paper and the comic strip.

Step 9. You can read the comic strip by holding it up to the mirror.

Turpentine can be a dangerous liquid to use. Be very careful not to get it in your eyes. It can also be very irritating to the skin of some people. Be sure to wash your hands after using it. It can be harmful to some surfaces, too. Be sure to protect the objects around you from coming in contact with it.

Specific gravity is found by dividing the weight of a substance by the weight of an equal amount of water. Specific gravity of a liquid is measured with a hydrometer. The specific gravity or density of water is 1.0. The specific gravity of other substances are measured in numbers compared to water and its specific gravity of 1.

17

It was a Sunday afternoon in early October. I stumbled into the house from a backpacking trip with the Scouts on the Appalachian Trail.

I was exhausted. All I could think of was bed and sleep. My mom said that Paul had called several times during the weekend even though she told him I would not be home until late Sunday afternoon.

I phoned him to find out what was so important.

"My science teacher told me to make a chemical volcano for class on Monday. I have no idea how to make a chemical volcano or even what one is. I went to the library, but all of the chemistry experiment books were checked out. Since I just came to this school last month, you're the only one I know who can help me."

"There's not much of a mystery to making a chemical volcano," I said. "I will explain to you how to do it.

"Talk to the teacher at the beginning of class. You may be able to get her permission to do yours outdoors. If you can do it outdoors, you may get a better grade, because it will be more authentic and more impressive than anyone else's."

In the experiment the baking soda, a base, and vinegar, an acid, react together releasing carbon dioxide. Because carbon dioxide gas is heavier than air it pushes the air out of the bottle. The detergent helps make more bubbles. The food coloring makes the experiment even more spectacular.

These are the same instructions I gave to Paul.

HOW TO MAKE
A CHEMICAL VOLCANO

EQUIPMENT

Note: For best results do this experiment out of doors in the dirt. If this is not possible do it in the sink.

1 narrow-neck bottle (25 oz./750 ml)
a mound of dirt
1 tablespoon liquid detergent
few drops red food coloring
1 cup vinegar (acetic acid, CH_3COOH)
warm water (H_2O)
2 tablespoons baking soda (sodium bicarbonate, $NaHCO_3$)

EXPERIMENT

Step 1. Set the bottle on the ground and build up a mound of dirt around it so that only the neck of the bottle shows a little.
Step 2. Put 1 tablespoon liquid detergent in the bottle.

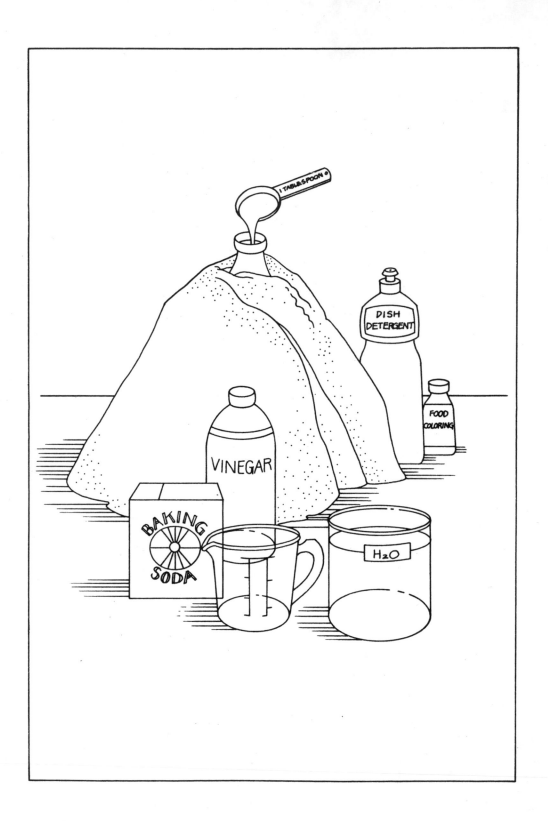

Step 3. Add a few drops of food coloring.

Step 4. Add 1 cup vinegar.

Step 5. Add warm water, enough to fill the bottle almost to the top.

Step 6. Very quickly add 2 tablespoons baking soda that has been mixed with a little water. Mixing it with water makes it easier to add it quickly.

18

One Thursday evening I rode my bike to my friend Josh's house. I was very anxious to see the coin collection he had been talking about. I came to a skidding halt on the driveway just as Josh's father opened the garage door.

He said to me, "Hello there, Alan. I've never seen you in such a hurry. Did you leave any of your chemicals here?"

"No, not this time," I replied. "I'm here to see Josh's famous coin collection."

With that Josh called to me from the window of his room, and I ran in to meet him. As we were looking at his coin collection, Josh said to me, "I am thinking of selling my collection to a coin dealer. With your knowledge of chemistry is there anything you know of that would make my old coins shiny? The better they look the more money I will get."

"Sure," I replied, "I can tell you how to improve the appearance of your copper and silver coins. Let's go down to your kitchen and see if we can find the supplies we need."

Before you try the two experiments I should explain the mysterious reactions that take place.

Do you know what causes silver to become tarnished? The silver reacts with the sulfur dioxide in the air to form silver sulfide, which is tarnish. The heated solution of baking soda, salt, and water is an electrolyte. An electrolyte is a liquid that carries an electric current between two electrodes. The electrolyte solution reacts with the silver sulfide causing the sulfur to leave the silver and unite with the aluminum to form aluminum sulfide. This explains the fact that the aluminum foil becomes tarnished.

In the copper-plating experiment the vinegar and salt work together. The acid in the vinegar loosens the dirt on the penny, and the salt, acting as an abrasive when the jar is shaken, removes the dirt from the surface. When this happens some of the copper also comes off with the dirt. In the second part of the experiment, some of the iron in the nail reacts with the vinegar and the salt and goes into solution. The iron going into solution makes the copper come out of solution and coat the nail. Simply explained, the salt and vinegar cause some of the iron and copper to trade places.

THE CASE OF THE VANISHING SILVER TARNISH

EQUIPMENT

large pan (like a roasting pan)
aluminum foil
water (H_2O)
1 teaspoon salt (sodium chloride, $NaCl$)
1 tablespoon baking soda (sodium bicarbonate, $NaHCO_3$)

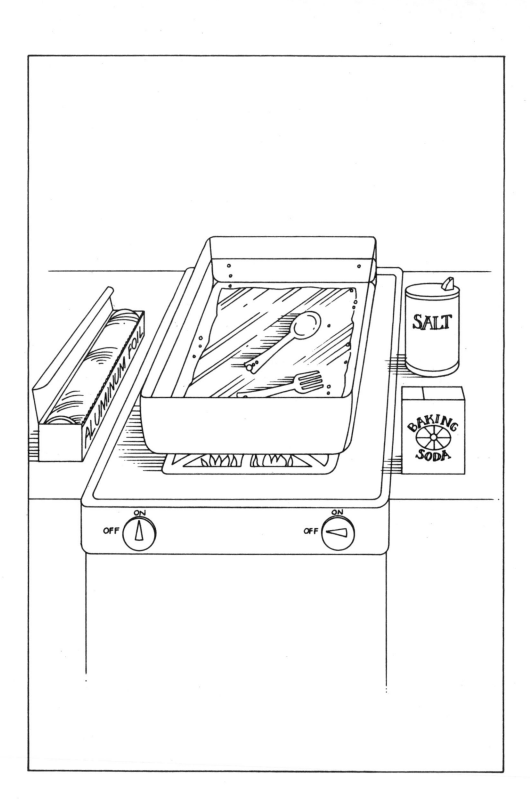

tarnished silver (silver sulfide, AgS), for example, a piece of jewelry *without* stones

or a quarter minted before 1964 (most coins minted after 1964 are made of copper with nickel plating)

or a fork or spoon—no knives (stones in jewelry and knife blades will loosen in boiling water)

CAUTION stove

EXPERIMENT

Step 1. Line the pan with aluminum foil shiny side up.

Step 2. Fill the pan with water and add 1 teaspoon salt and 1 tablespoon baking soda.

Step 3. Add the piece of tarnished silver.

CAUTION Step 4. Heat on the stove.

Step 5. When the experiment is finished, remove the silver with tongs or allow to cool before removing it. Rinse with water and dry with a clean cloth.

Always have an adult help you when performing an experiment that requires you to use the stove.

THE SECRET OF COPPER PLATING

EQUIPMENT

10–20 pennies (depending on the size of the jar)

jar with lid

vinegar (acetic acid, CH_3COOH)

1 tablespoon salt (sodium chloride, NaCl)
iron nail

EXPERIMENT

Step 1. Put pennies in jar.
Step 2. Add 1 in. (2–3 cm) vinegar.
Step 3. Add 1 tablespoon salt.
Step 4. Put lid on jar and shake 10 times.
Step 5. Let it sit for 10 minutes.
Step 6. Observe.
Step 7. Add nail to the solution and let sit 30 minutes.
Step 8. Observe.

A friend of mine was really beginning to be a grouch. He stopped talking to people, was getting poor grades at school, and was starting to lose his friends. Finally one day when I was at his house his mother said to him, "What has gotten into you? You've become impossible to live with. And another thing, the dentist's bill has skyrocketed. How did you manage to get eleven cavities?"

"Well, Mom, I think I have a bad disease," he replied. "It all started one night about a month ago. I walked into my room in the dark to get a book. I was chewing on some wintergreen candy. I happened to glance at the mirror, and I saw sparks in my mouth!"

"Well. . . . I never heard of anything like that in my life," said his mother. "Does that explain eleven cavities?"

"I have been trying all sorts of candies at night trying to find out what is wrong. I've discovered it only happens when I chew on wintergreen candy."

"I don't want to interrupt," I said. "But, anyone can do that if they chew wintergreen candy. That is a phenomenon known as triboluminescence."

MYSTICAL MOUTH LIGHTNING

EQUIPMENT

dark room
mirror
wintergreen Life-Saver

EXPERIMENT

Step 1. Stand in front of a mirror in a dark room.
Step 2. Bite down on a wintergreen Life-Saver. Keep your mouth open at the same time and observe closely in the mirror the side of your mouth where you have the Life-Saver.

When the sucrose, or sugar, crystals break up under pressure (from the teeth biting down on them), positive and negative electrical charges separate. The difference in charge causes electrons to jump across the gap in order to neutralize the total charge. The electrons cause the nitrogen in the air to emit blue-white light. The sparks that are emitted or given off by the sugar are identical to lightning! Normally this release of voltage cannot be seen. But wintergreen in the candies enhances the effect, because one of the properties of wintergreen is that it *fluoresces.* Fluorescence is a process in which a substance absorbs energy and then emits the excess energy in the form of blue-green light.

20

One hot June day my cousin, Michael, called.

"I'm going to camp next week, Alan," he said. "The last night at camp, each cabin is expected to entertain the others around the camp fire. Do you know of any experiments I could do for entertainment?"

"You caught me just in time, Michael, I leave for camp tomorrow. I know of three egg experiments you can do. They require a stove, because the eggs must be hard boiled," I replied.

"I don't think that will be a problem," Mike said. "I can either get them hard boiled in the kitchen at dinner time, or I can probably boil them over the camp fire."

"Since you're not leaving for camp until next week, you have loads of time to get your supplies together and even practice the experiments before you go," I said.

These are the three mysterious eggs-periments that Mike did at camp.

THE MYSTERY OF
THE FLOATING EGG

EQUIPMENT

AUTION stove
egg
saucepan
water (H_2O)
spoon
jar (8 oz./240 ml)
approximately 3 teaspoons salt (sodium chloride, NaCl)

EXPERIMENT

AUTION Step 1. Hard boil the egg. (Cook it in a saucepan of water for 15 minutes.)
Step 2. After the egg is cooked, lift the hot egg out of the saucepan with a spoon and put it in the jar.
Step 3. Fill the jar three-quarters full of water.
Step 4. Observe the position of the egg, then remove it.
Step 5. Add 3 teaspoons salt to the jar and replace the egg.
Step 6. Observe the egg. If no change has occurred, add more salt 1 teaspoon at a time.

Have an adult prepare the egg for you or supervise while you prepare it.

The egg is heavier than the water so it sinks. When salt is added to the water it forms a heavier solution. The heavier salt solution gives the egg more support, and the egg is buoyed up by the saline solution with the result that the egg floats.

THE BAFFLING
BOUNCING EGG

EQUIPMENT

CAUTION stove
egg
saucepan
water (H_2O)
spoon
jar with lid
vinegar (acetic acid, CH_3COOH)

EXPERIMENT

CAUTION Step 1. Hard boil the egg. (Cook it in a saucepan of water for 15 minutes.)

Step 2. After the egg is cooked put it into the jar using the spoon.

Step 3. Fill the jar with vinegar.

Step 4. Put the lid on the jar and let it sit for 24 hours.

Step 5. At the end of the 24 hours, remove the egg from the jar and observe.

Step 6. Try bouncing the egg on the table.

Have an adult cook the egg for you or supervise while you are cooking it.

The acid (vinegar) dissolved the shell of the egg. The egg absorbed some of the vinegar and the egg became very rubbery.

Save the egg if you are going to try out the Third Mysterious Eggs-periment.

99 /

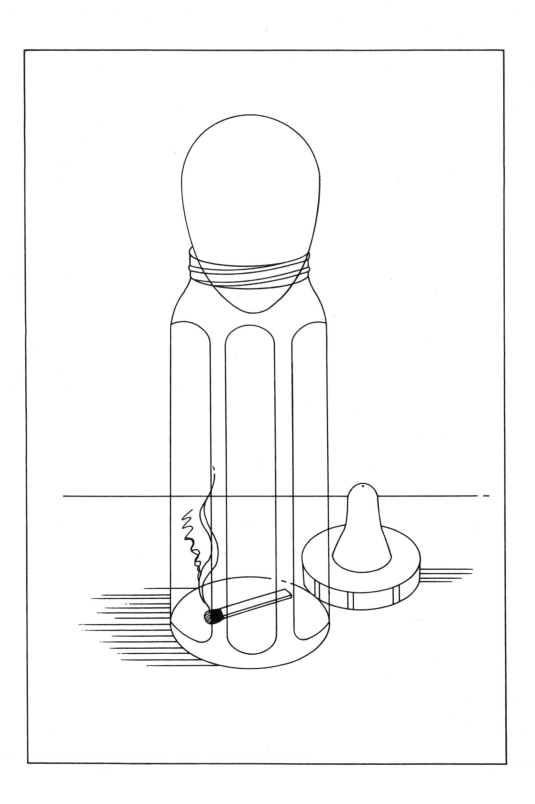

A THIRD MYSTERIOUS
EGGS-PERIMENT

Note: Do this experiment after the Baffling Bouncing Egg Experiment. If you damaged the egg in that experiment, then you will have to prepare another egg in the same way.

EQUIPMENT

baby bottle

CAUTION match

hard-boiled egg that has been soaked in vinegar

EXPERIMENT

Step 1. Make sure that the egg is just slightly bigger than the bottle opening.

Step 2. Drop a lighted match into the baby bottle.

Step 3. Quickly place the egg, small end down, in the mouth of the bottle.

Have an adult with you when you use the lighted match.

If the egg was sucked into the bottle when you did the experiment, it was because the gases in the bottle cooled and contracted after the match went out, and a partial vacuum was formed pulling or sucking the egg into the bottle.

21

The Puzzling Case of the Wax Mountains experiment is a fascinating way to detect differences in the weights of liquids.

Since it is the last experiment in the book, you, "the detective of chemistry," should be experienced enough to solve the case of the puzzling mountain formation. A clue can be found in one of the sentences above.

How cold does the water have to be?

Try the experiment with ice water.
Try it with warm water.
Does the temperature of the water make a difference in the success or failure of your experiment?

Did you deduce the explanation for this puzzling case? Because wax is lighter than water, it rises up in peaks as it cools.

THE PUZZLING CASE
OF THE WAX MOUNTAINS

EQUIPMENT

double boiler or simmer ring and saucepan
water (H_2O)
candle stubs of various colors
CAUTION stove
large spoon
piece of plywood 6 × 8 in. (15 × 20 cm)
potholder
large pan (size of a roasting pan) filled with cold water

EXPERIMENT

Step 1. If you use the double-boiler method, fill the bottom pan with water and put one candle in the top portion. Place the top portion on top of the bottom and heat it on the stove. If you use the simmer ring and saucepan, put the simmer ring on the stove burner, place the saucepan on top of it, and put the candle in the pan.

CAUTION Step 2. Heat until the candle melts.

Step 3. Lift out the candle wick with the large spoon.

CAUTION Step 4. Using a potholder, pour the wax over the piece of wood.

Step 5. Immediately immerse the wood into the large pan of cold water. Be sure not to tilt the wood as you put it into the pan.

Step 6. Quickly remove the wood from the water.

Step 7. On the same piece of wood, repeat steps 1 through 6 for each different color candle that you have.

Always have an adult with you when you use the stove.

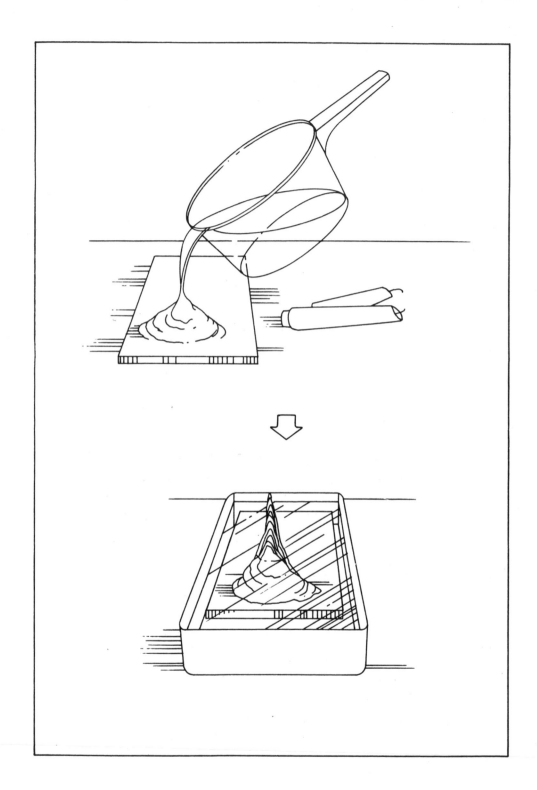

Do not pour wax onto the wood over the sink. If wax gets down the drain it will clog it. It will be even more disastrous if your sink has a garbage disposal.

Remember this wax is very hot—do not pour it onto the wood near the end where your fingers are holding the wood.

BIBLIOGRAPHY

Allison, Linda, and David Katz. *Gee, Whiz!*. New York: Little, Brown and Co., 1983.

Amer, Heather. *The Know How Book of Experiments.* St. Paul: EMC Corp., 1978.

Ardley, Neil. *Working with Water.* New York: Franklin Watts, Inc., 1982.

Arnov, Boris. *Water: Experiments to Understand It.* New York: Lothrop, Lee & Shepard Books, 1980.

Beeler, Nelson F., and Franklyn M. Branley. *Experiments in Chemistry.* New York: Thomas Y. Crowell Co., 1952.

Brown, Bob. *200 Science Experiments for Boys and Girls.* New York: William Collins and World Publishing Co., 1973.

Brown, Robert J. *333 Science Tricks and Experiments.* Blue Ridge Summit, Pa.: Tab Books, Inc., 1984.

Cherrier, François. *Fascinating Experiments in Chemistry.* New York: Sterling Pub. Co., 1978.

Cobb, Vicki. *Chemically Active! Experiments You Can Do at Home.* New York: J. B. Lippincott, 1985.

Freeman, Mae, and Ira Freeman. *Fun with Chemistry,* rev. ed. New York: Random House, 1962.

Gardner, Martin. *Entertaining Science Experiments with Everyday Objects.* New York: Dover Publications, 1957.

Gardner, Robert. *Kitchen Chemistry.* New York: Julian Messner Co., 1982.

Goldstein-Jackson, Kevin. *Experiments with Everyday Objects.* Englewood Cliffs, N.J.: Prentice Hall, Inc., 1978.

Herbert, Don. *Mr. Wizard's Supermarket Science.* New York: Random House, 1980.

Hobben, Dorothy. *Science Experiments That Really Work.* Chicago: Follett Pub. Co., 1970.

Johnson, Mary. *Pocket Scientist Chemistry Experiments.* London: Usborne Pub. Ltd., 1981.

Johnston, Ted. *Science Magic with Chemistry and Biology.* New York: Arco Publishing Co., 1975.

Lehane, M.S. *Science Tricks.* New York: Franklin Watts, Inc., 1980.

McGill, Ormond. *Science Magic.* New York: Arco Publishing Co., 1984.

Morgan, Alfred. *First Chemistry Book for Boys and Girls.* New York: Charles Scribner's Sons, 1977.

————. *Simple Chemical Experiments.* New York: Meredith Press, 1941.

Ontario Science Center. *Science Works: 65 Experiments that Introduce the Fun and Wonder of Science.* Reading, Mass.: Addison-Wesley Publishing Co., Inc., 1984.

Sholit, Nathan. *Cup and Saucer Chemistry.* New York: Grosset & Dunlap, Inc., 1972.

Unesco Source Books for Teaching. *700 Science Experiments for Everyone.* Garden City, N.Y.: Doubleday and Co., Inc., 1956.

Vowles, Andrew. *EDC Book of Amazing Experiments You Can Do at Home.* Tulsa: EDC Pub., 1985.

Walters, Derek. *Science World Chemistry.* New York: Franklin Watts, Inc., 1982.

Watson, Philip. *Liquid Magic.* New York: Lothrop, Lee & Shepard Books, 1982.

White, Laurence B., Jr. *Investigating Science with Rubber Bands.* Reading, Mass.: Addison-Wesley Publishing Co., Inc., 1969.

INDEX

ABOUT
THE AUTHOR

Alan Kramer is a thirteen-year-old
middle school student with a long-
standing interest in chemistry.

He began writing this book at age
nine while a student at the Bushy
Park Elementary School in Howard
County, Maryland.

He lives in Cooksville, Maryland.